Beginner's Guide to
Crewel Embroidery

To my ever-loving
and very patient
husband, Eric

Beginner's Guide to
Crewel Embroidery

Jane Rainbow

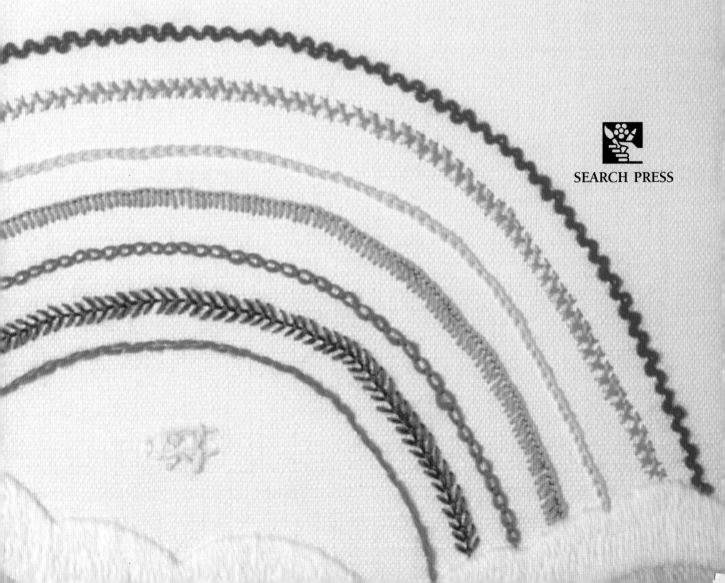

SEARCH PRESS

First published in Great Britain 1999

Search Press Limited
Wellwood, North Farm Road,
Tunbridge Wells, Kent TN2 3DR

Reprinted 2000, 2002, 2003, 2004, 2006, 2007, 2009, 2010

Text copyright © Jane Rainbow 1999
Embroidery designs copyright © Jane Rainbow 1999

Photographs by Search Press Studios
Photographs and design copyright © Search Press Ltd. 1999

ISBN 978 0 85532 869 6

The Publishers and author can accept no responsibility for any
consequences arising from the information, advice or instructions
given in this publication.

Readers are permitted to reproduce any of the items/patterns in
this book for their personal use, or for the purposes of selling for
charity, free of charge and without the prior permission of the
Publishers. Any use of the items/patterns for commercial purposes
is not permitted without the prior permission of the Publishers.

Suppliers
If you have difficulty in obtaining any of the materials and
equipment mentioned in this book, please visit the Search Press
website for details of suppliers:
www.searchpress.com

Alternatively, should you require further information about Jane
Rainbow's frames, kits (which include many of the designs
featured in this book) or classes, please send a stamped addressed
envelope (or pre-paid international postal coupons if enquiring
from outside the UK) to the author at: 1 Landgate Mews, Well
Lane, Stow-on-the-Wold, Gloucestershire, GL54 1DE.

Publisher's note
All the step-by-step photographs in this book feature the
author, Jane Rainbow, demonstrating crewel embroidery. No
models have been used.

Printed in Malaysia by Times Offset (M) Sdn Bhd

I would like to thank all at Search Press,
especially Roz for persuading me to say yes;
Chantal for keeping me sane; and Lotti for her
tolerance.

I would also like to thank Peter Greville for
encouraging me to enter the crewel market some
fifteen years ago; Jim Moeller for being such
a good friend; and Juliet Lovatt for finishing
Arcadia in time.

Finally, a big thank you for all the encouragement
and support of my pupils and friends.

Contents

INTRODUCTION

To embroider is to embellish or adorn by means of a needle. (It is also described in the dictionary as unnecessary or extravagant ornament!) Crewel embroidery is a type of surface embroidery worked only in crewel wool. It is the most traditional of English embroideries, and that is why I love it.

Crewel wool is a two-ply worsted wool or yarn. As a result of being worked in wool, crewel embroidery is much thicker and heavier than other types of embroidery, and the stitching lies above the background fabric – not just on it. If a design is embroidered in any other thread, such as silk or cotton for example, it is called surface embroidery *not* crewel embroidery. However, exactly the same stitches and techniques are used. So, if you are not happy working with wool, feel free to work all my designs in threads of your choice . . . but

remember never to call your work crewel embroidery! Crewel embroidery has been in existence for more than ten centuries and, generally, it becomes fashionable about every fifty years. It was especially popular during the mid-seventeenth century and is often referred to as Jacobean embroidery. The most famous early piece is the Bayeux Tapestry, in which pictorial panels depict the battle of 1066 between the Britons and Normans. But let me have my soap-box again: technically, a tapestry is woven on a loom with a shuttle and has nothing to do with embroidery or needles. The majority of large wall hangings seen in stately homes are true tapestries and are woven. Embroidery worked on a canvas is also often called a tapestry, but it should be referred to as canvas embroidery.

I have been stitching surface embroidery for almost fifty years. I started age six and one of the saving graces of being sent away to a typical English girls' boarding school for eight years was that we had an excellent embroidery and needlework teacher. I owe a lot to 'Aunt' Read. She taught me wonderful basic techniques but more importantly to enjoy unpicking. There is absolutely no point in taking up a piece of embroidery unless you enjoy going in reverse! The best embroiderers seem to unpick three times as much as they work! However, the joy of crewel is that it is often possible to cheat.

As an embroidery teacher, I have often found that many of my pupils want me beside them at home. As a result, I have made a two-and-a-half-hour video on basic techniques that has become very popular around the world. Now the time has come to put pen to paper and to share my knowledge with those of you who prefer to read rather than use a video recorder! There are many amongst you who will find this type of embroidery easy. However, anyone who has worked only counted or canvas embroidery may find it a little more difficult to be 'free'. There is no counting involved. You dictate to the fabric rather than the fabric dictating to you. Hopefully, my book will help you to be a bold and free stitcher.

Finally, I am never happy with the terms crewel or canvas *work*. It makes it sound like a chore or a boring task. Canvas work conjures up a picture of prisoners making mail bags or people working in sail lofts. Embroidery should be a joy and a pleasure, and I hope that after reading my book, you will agree. Remember to enjoy every stitch. It really does not matter how long it takes to finish – it is the pleasure in doing rather than finishing that matters. Welcome to the creweler's world.

Design

I meet up with so many people who either cannot or do not want to design their own embroidery projects. It really is important to understand that you do not have to be artistic to be an embroiderer – there are so many wonderful kits on the market.

However, if you do not want to work from a kit but are unable to design, why not take one of the beautiful linen union furnishing fabrics as your starting point. These are widely available and there are lots of designs to choose from (although you should be aware of copyright laws and restrictions if making embroideries for commercial purposes). You can embroider over the printed design and even embroider out areas that you want to hide, using a colour that matches the background.

If you want to be more creative you can look for design ideas from many different sources. I have collected lots of ideas from historical pieces over the years. I also hoard cuttings from magazines, greetings cards, wrapping paper, wallpaper and fabric. Train yourself to be observant. If you are good with a still camera, you can even take photographs of things that inspire you.

When planning a design, you need to consider what size it should be. Think also about proportion. Remember that the space you leave out should complement the design – it is just as important as the design itself. It is also a good idea to decide upon what form the finished embroidery will take. As it is much cheaper to buy readymade picture frames, stools and cushion pads, this is the stage at which you need to decide the final measurements of your project.

During the initial period of preparing a design, I work only in black and white. Generally, I hang it on the wall in a spot I pass often, and each time I look at it I check that I am truly happy with the proportions. When I am entirely happy with the composition, I choose my colours and transfer the design to the fabric (see page 16–17). I am then ready to start stitching.

Avalon

Composition and proportion are essential components of a good design. The colours you choose can also change the feel of a design totally. This stunning panel could be used as a picture or a firescreen.

Materials & equipment

Fabric

Crewel embroidery requires a furnishing weight fabric, rather than a dress weight one. Ideally, the fabric should be made of fifty per cent linen. This has many advantages, one of which is that the fabric has spring. When you pull a thick needle through it, the hole springs open but it will also spring shut around the stitch. If you work on a pure cotton fabric that has no give, you will get sore fingers from pulling the needle through, and holes at the base of the stitches. Fabric with an element of linen in it can also be stroked back into place around the stitches, where necessary. Finally, once you have finished stitching, the natural linen starches that are already in the fabric will come to life and crisp up the fabric during the stretching or blocking process!

Traditionally, crewel was worked on a hundred per cent linen twill, but this does not wear as well as linen and cotton union and is twice as costly and usually not as wide. Most linen union fabrics have ten or twelve per cent manmade fibre content, and the rest are made up equally of linen and cotton. They are available in a wide range of colours. If you are having problems finding them, ask in your local furnishing store for linen and cotton union fabrics.

When cutting the fabric, remember to allow enough turnings beyond the design for making up, and also allow for the embroidery frame you are using. I generally add at least 12.5cm (5in) to my design area, but as I always need at least 52.5cm x 32.5cm (21 x 13in) for my frame, this influences the final cutting.

Seal the raw edges of the fabric with either overlocking or blanket stitch, masking tape or seam binding. Iron out any creases using a hot steam iron, before transferring the design on to the fabric.

Linen union fabrics are available in a range of colours, including blue, green, cream and gold. Threads (see page 14) should be chosen to work with your background colour to enhance the design.

Threads

There are various types of crewel wool on the market. They vary in thickness, texture, twist and hairiness! My preference is for the type known as Persian wool. It was originally spun especially for the Persian carpet repairers. It comes as three loosely wound two-ply strands, in 7.2m (8yd) skeins and 125g (4oz) hanks which equal approximately twenty-one

Persian crewel wool

English crewel wool

Fine English crewel wool

French crewel wool

skeins. There are four hundred and seventeen shades available in the Persian wool range and it has a natural lustre that gives an embroidery a silky appearance. All other wools tend to have a matt quality, and so they absorb light rather than reflect it.

The availability of wools varies considerably around the world. I will therefore not specify brands or shade numbers of the threads in this book, but leave it up to you to choose your own. Where I give quantities, these are in skeins and amount to 7.2m (8yd) of three strands, which is equivalent to 21.6m (24yd).

Needles

I always use a No. 4 crewel needle – an English-made one! This has a long eye and a sharp point. I also use a No. 20 tapestry needle for some stitches.

No. 4 crewel needle
No. 22 chenille needle
No. 20 tapestry needle

If you have difficulty threading a crewel needle, try using a chenille needle – this is similar to a tapestry needle, with a larger eye and sharp point. I would recommend a No. 20 or 22.

Frames

I find it essential to work crewel embroidery on a frame. It is very much easier to make good stitches if the fabric is held taut. If the frame is held or supported so that you have both hands free, this is better still.

Embroidery hoops or ring frames

These are available in different sizes, and in wood, plastic or metal. I prefer the deeper wooden ones and would choose a 15cm (6in) frame (or smaller) if I was holding it in my hand. The hoop should only be held by the frame and your fingers should not push up on the fabric. It does not matter if you crush the embroidery in the hoop, it will all come back to shape during the stretching process.

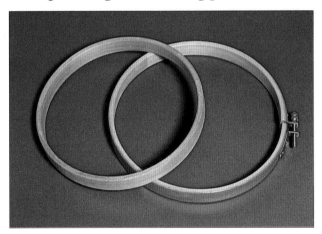

Note If you are working on fabric that has a linen content, you will get a permanent hoop mark if you leave the material in the frame overnight! It is therefore imperative that you always remove an embroidery from a hoop or ring frame at the end of each session of stitching.

Pin frame

I have used a pin frame for over thirty-five years. This type of frame is a copy of a medieval embroidery frame.

The frame itself is made of wood. The wood is upholstered, and the work is attached to the padding with pins. You should pin on the outside of the upholstery, pointing the pins towards the centre. You will need to use a different thickness of pin depending on the weight of the canvas or fabric used: the finer the fabric, the finer the pin. The joy of this type of frame is that you can work on any size of embroidery. Simply pin the area you need to stitch over the frame. If the work is larger than the frame, unpin each section as it is worked, move on, repin and continue working. Should your work be smaller than the frame, attach scrap material to enlarge it to the required size. Another advantage of a pin frame is that you can leave the work on it for any period of time.

Other items

Pens You will need a black felt-tip pen for tracing the design, and a water-erasable felt-tip pen for marking the design on to fabric.

Tracing paper This is used for transferring a design on to fabric.

Rule or tape measure This is used for measuring fabric and for positioning a design precisely.

Masking tape Use 2.5cm (1in) wide masking tape to cover the raw edges of fabric. Masking tape is also useful for securing a tracing to your surface when transferring a design on to fabric.

Scissors Large dressmakers' scissors are required for cutting fabric. Fine, sharp embroidery scissors should be used for cutting threads. You will also need paper-cutting scissors for cutting graph paper, paper for designs and tracing paper.

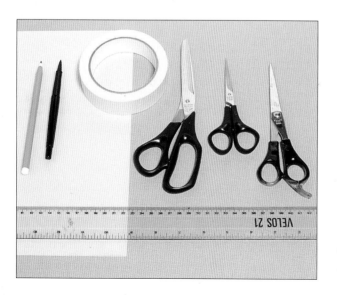

Stretching materials

Wooden board This should be at least 1.25cm (½in) thick. It is best not to use either a very hard or a very soft wood, as nails need to be inserted. Block board is ideal. Whatever board you use, it must be at least 5cm (2in) bigger than the fabric you want to stretch on it. If you are an embroidery addict, it is worth investing in a board at least 1m (40in) square.

2.5cm (1in) nails These are used to secure the fabric to the board.

Hammer Nails are hammered into the board and removed with a hammer. Choose a claw-type hammer if possible.

Graph paper This is used as a guide to ensure that the edges of the fabric are straight. It is essential for accurate stretching. Dressmaker's graph paper is excellent.

Mist sprayer A mist sprayer is an excellent way of ensuring that the fabric is dampened but not saturated with water.

The work station

It is important to consider where and how you sit whilst embroidering. Try to ensure that you have good spinal support, and avoid spending hours crouched over a frame. Choose a frame that is adjustable to the height you need, so you are able to sit with your spine as straight as possible. Also, take care of your eyes. Work with a light directed on to your embroidery, but remember to look up and refocus your eyes often! I use my pin frame for all types of embroidery, including cross stitch, canvas, quilting and surface embroidery. I use a Lowery Workstand and a magnifier and lamp on a clamp. If I am working with a hoop or ring frame, I often choose a 20cm (8in) seat or chair frame (see top left of photograph). When using this, I can sit in a comfortable chair with the embroidery held in my lap and work with both hands freely. This type is also available with a clamp for a table, or free-standing on the floor.

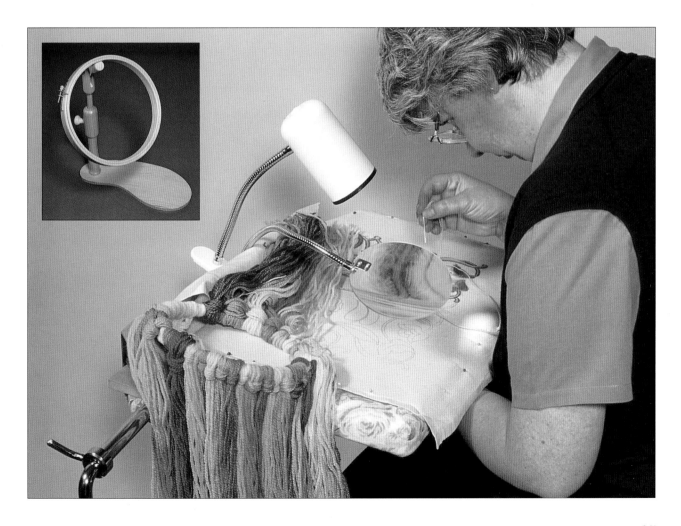

Getting started

Transferring a design

Before you begin tracing a design, you need to ensure that the design you wish to use is the correct size. Some of the patterns in this book are not full-size, so you will need to enlarge them using a photocopier. A photocopier also allows you to make the designs smaller than they were worked originally.

I find it best to work with a tracing of the design rather than a photocopy of it. This is because the linen fabric on which I mostly work, is quite thick. Tracing paper, rather than photocopy paper, enables as much light as possible to shine through the fabric when transferring the design.

I would suggest that you always use a water-erasable pen to trace your designs on to fabric. This means that any outline not covered by stitches will disappear during the washing and/or stretching process.

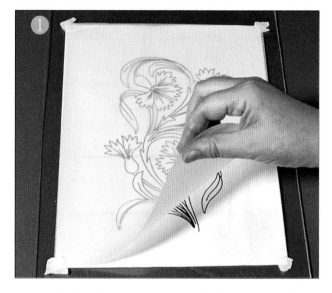

1. Attach the design to a piece of glass or a window with small pieces of masking tape. Attach a piece of tracing paper over the design.

2. Trace around the outline of the design with a black felt-tip pen. Remove the design.

3. Cut your fabric to the required size and place masking tape over the raw edges.

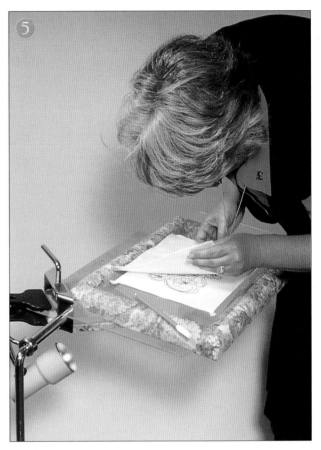

5. With a light source behind the design, trace the image on to the fabric using a water-erasable felt-tip pen.

> *Note* With an artificial light, or natural sunlight, behind the design you will be able to trace it on to fabric easily. If it is a sunny day, you can attach the tracing and the fabric to a window – the light will shine through and make the design line clear.

4. Place the fabric over the tracing. Stick in place with masking tape.

Framing-up

There are lots of different types of frame available, all of which require different ways of framing up. In the following demonstrations, I show how to frame-up a hoop and a pin frame. Whichever frame you are framing up, the most important thing is to ensure that the fabric ends up drum tight.

Embroidery hoop

An embroidery hoop is one of the quickest and easiest frames to use. However, at the end of your embroidery session, you may need a screw driver to release the screw to take the frame apart.

1. Position your fabric over the inner hoop.

Note If the outer hoop pushes down too easily over the fabric, remove it, tighten the screw on the outer ring, and try again.

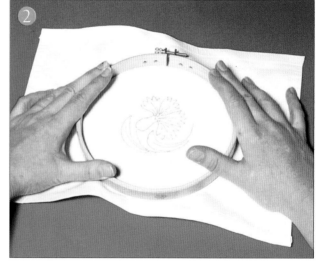

2. Screw the outer hoop fairly tight, then force it over the inner hoop to pull the fabric taut.

Pin frame

One of the many advantages of a pin frame is that it is quick and easy to attach and detach the embroidery to and from the frame – you can therefore use the same frame for more than one project. A pin frame is easily balanced in your arms or against a table, so it can be used without a special stand.

> *Note* If you are working on fabric larger than the frame, pin up the area you want to embroider, then roll up and pin the excess.

1. Place the fabric over the frame. Pin one corner, then the adjacent corners, then the fourth, diagonally opposite corner.

2. Pin the centre side. Continue until all the centre sides are pinned.

> *Note* When you are pinning, pull the fabric taut and place the pins on the outside of the frame, rather than on the top edge, and point them in towards the centre of the frame.

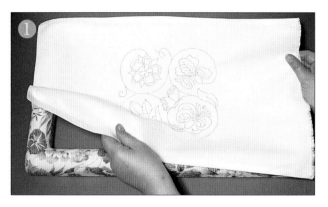

3. Pin half way between the centre pin and corner pins.

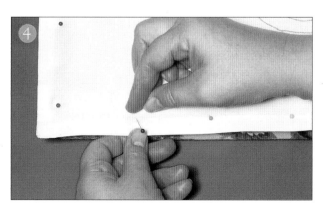

4. Repeat, pinning half way between two pins until the whole frame is pinned.

Preparing your threads

When working with crewel wool, it is best to work with lengths no longer than 37cm (15in). However, I find that the Persian crewel wool is so strong, I can work with double this length.

You can keep lengths of wool looped on a vacant embroidery hoop, a hole-punched piece of card, or a coat hanger. If there is more than one shade of a colour, keep these together and in order of darkness.

1. Remove the label and unravel the wool. Place the two ends together.

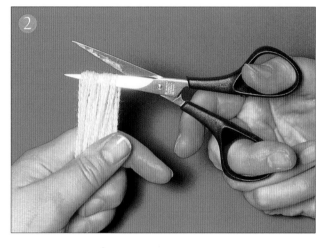

2. Fold in half, then half again, and continue until you have a satisfactory working length. Cut through all the loops to create separate lengths of wool.

3. Loop the prepared skein of wool on to the frame.

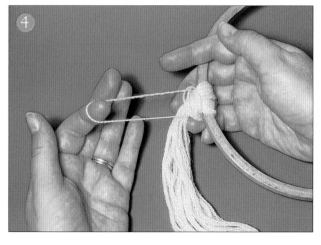

4. To remove a single strand of wool, simply pull one from the loop of the knot.

Threading a needle

This can cause some nightmares! The method I use means that you are not threading the wool through the eye of the needle, but threading the needle over the wool.

This is a wonderfully simple and very effective way of threading a needle, but remember . . . practice makes perfect! Persevere, and you will soon be able to thread a needle with your eyes shut!

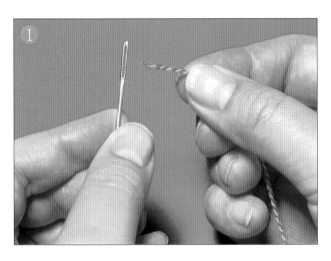

1. Take the needle in your lesser hand, and the thread in your major hand.

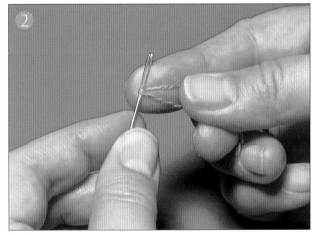

2. Wrap the thread around the eye of the needle and pinch it between your finger and thumb. Remove the needle and keep the fold of thread squeezed between your finger and thumb so that it is firmly pinched and you can feel where it is but not see it. With your fingers still pinching the thread, pass the eye of the needle over the fold of thread.

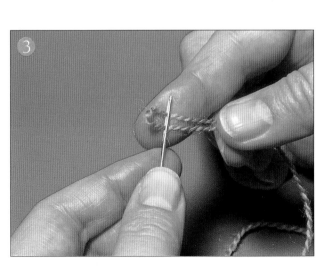

3. Pass the fold of the thread through the eye of the needle.

Note Avoid opening your squeezed fingers too much when passing the needle over the wool.

Beginning and ending your threads

When you look at a finished piece of embroidery, your eye tends to look at the centre first, then upwards. Therefore, the most insignificant area will be towards the bottom. All embroiderers' stitching improves with practise, so do not put your first attempts at a project in the most eye-catching spot!

Traditionally, it was thought that if you did not start in the centre, you would ruin the tension. As all crewel embroidery tension problems get sorted out in the stretching process, experience has taught me that it is not essential to start in the middle and work outwards. I would certainly tend to start with leaves rather than flowers, stalks rather than leaves, but feel free to find your own path.

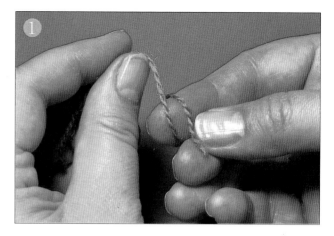

1. To tie a knot in the end of a thread, wrap the thread once around your forefinger.

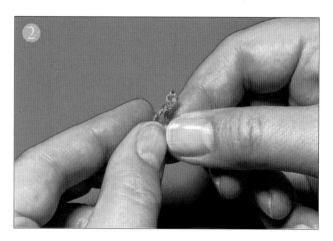

2. Roll the thread towards you.

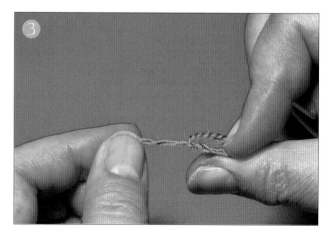

3. Tighten the knot.

4. Place the knot approximately 2cm (¾in) from where you want the first stitch to be. Bring the needle up, making sure that the thread on the back is going across an area to be worked.

Note The knot can be placed in open background. The thread on the back must be crossing an area of the design that is to be stitched solidly. In this way, the thread can be caught in when embroidering.

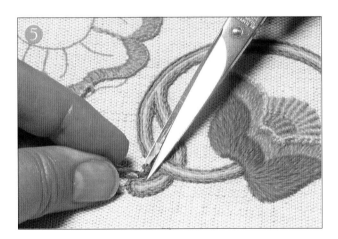

5. When you have finished your stitching, cut off the knot.

6. To finish off, turn the fabric over and weave the needle several times into the threads. Cut off the end.

Note Occasionally, it may be necessary to leave an extra long starting thread so as to be able to rethread this and then weave it into the back.

EMBROIDERY STITCHES

This book contains only twelve crewel embroidery stitches. The carnation design supplied in this section has been worked as three different panels using various stitches and colours. As carnations look like ballet skirts, I have called the three variations *Giselle*, *Coppelia* and *Sylvia*. The carnation design is also worked as one design (*Les Sylphides*), incorporating all three variations and using yet another colour scheme. I hope that this will enable you to assess the different effects of colour and texture.

There are of course many more surface embroidery stitches. Hopefully, these designs will encourage further stitching. I have deliberately kept the number of different stitches used low, to show how effective this type of embroidery can be.

I work all my stitches from the outside in, from top to bottom, or as the sap flows back down to the roots. I find this helps the flow of the design. All the instructions that follow presume you have attached your starting thread appropriately (see pages 22–23).

Paradise

This colourful panel emphasises the joy of crewel embroidery, with its flowing design. It incorporates all the stitches featured in the book.

Pattern for the designs featured on pages 27, 32, 40 and 47

Giselle

This section introduces you to four stitches – stem stitch, chain stitch, split stitch and satin stitch. Once you have mastered the stitches, you will be able to work this flowing design.

Giselle

Design size
12.5 x 21cm (5 x 8½in)

Colours
1 skein each of two shades of pink and three shades of green
1 strand of wool was used throughout

Stitches
The calyx (base of the flower head) of each flower is worked in stem stitch – those on the larger flowers are in dark green and those on the smaller ones are in mid green. The outline is worked first, then the rows are filled in with stem stitch. Each row is worked in the same direction.

The flowers and stems are worked in chain stitch – the larger flowers are in deep pink, the smaller ones are in pale pink and the stems are in dark green.

The leaves are worked using all three shades of green. Each leaf was outlined in split stitch first, then embroidered in satin stitch. The top left leaf has the top side worked in pale green and the lower side in mid-green. The remainder are in pale or mid-green, with the exception of the centre bottom leaf which is in dark green.

Stem stitch

This linear stitch is one that many people find easier to work in the hand and not on a frame. However, I make my best linear stitches on a frame! As crewel embroidery is a heavy form of stitching, it is important to have good fabric tension. The embroidery thread tension should be firm but not tight – each stitch should be neatly laid on to the fabric without gathering it, and the stitch should not wobble on the surface.

This demonstration shows a solid start, which would be suitable for the base of a leaf or flower. If you want to form a point, simply begin with a whole stitch rather than a half stitch.

When working parallel rows, make sure the twist of the rope formed by this stitch is identical in each row. Do not change the side that the wool is kept on part way along a row.

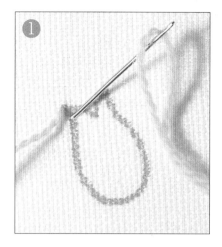

1. Work a half stitch.

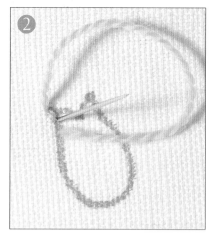

2. Bring the needle up at the beginning of the first half stitch.

Note Work a whole stitch to start, if you want to form a point (i.e. for a tendril). Then bring the needle up halfway between the first and second movements.

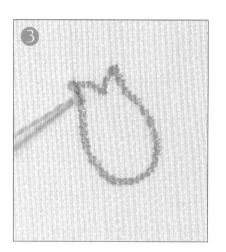

3. Pull the thread taut. Work a whole stitch and bring the needle up at the end of the first half stitch

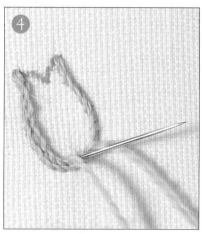

4. Repeat, working full stitches to complete the motif. Remember to keep the wool on the outside of the curve as you work.

Note Ideally, your stitching should be even. However, as curves become tighter, shorten your stitches so they do not fall over!

Chain stitch

This is another linear stitch, which again is often worked off a frame. It is best to work eight or nine stitches to 2.5cm (1in). Work all rows in the same direction.

This stitch has a pointed start and a blunt end, so consider this when planning where to begin.

If you are outlining a pointed petal in this stitch, step outside the loop when the point is complete, then come back up in the loop, change direction and continue.

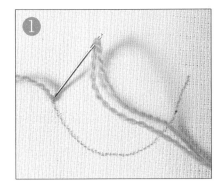

1. Come up at the point at which you want to start, then place the needle back down the same hole.

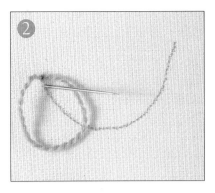

2. Come up about 3mm (1/8in) further along the design line, through the loop.

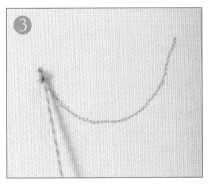

3. Pull the stitch taut, holding the thread horizontal to the fabric.

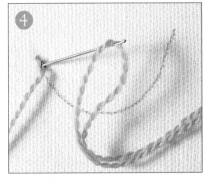

4. Go back through the same hole inside the loop to begin the next stitch (this makes the loop for the following stitch).

Note Should you need to join in a new thread whilst stitching chain stitch, leave the loop of the old thread on the front of the work, then attach the new thread and come up through the loop. Now tighten the old thread and finish it off, and continue with the new thread.

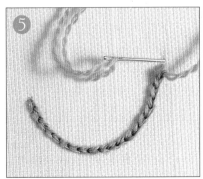

5. Repeat to outline the motif. To finish off, place the needle down outside the loop, making a small stitch to anchor the last link.

The outlines of these hearts are worked in chain stitch.

Split stitch

This is the last of the linear stitches, and it is frequently used to pad the edge of solid stitches: satin stitch, fly stitch and soft shading. In all the projects, you should work split stitch outlines around any area that is to be worked in these stitches.

This stitch will not be seen when the piece is finished, so generous stitches may be worked where curves will allow.

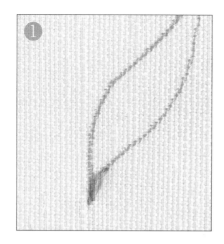

1. Work a straight stitch about 6mm (¼in) long to begin.

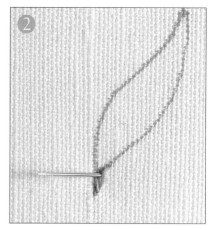

2. Bring the needle up a third of the way back along the straight stitch, to split the stitch.

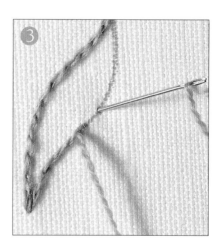

3. Repeat, to outline the motif.

Split stitch is used for padding the outlines of soft shading, satin and fly stitch.

Split stitch is worked underneath soft shading for the leaves and petals of this flower.

Satin stitch

Satin is the simplest stitch to work but probably the most difficult to get just right. Satin stitch is a collection of straight stitches tightly packed beside each other. I generally work about nine stitches to 1cm (³⁄₈in).

This stitch is most effective worked on an oblique angle. It is often helpful to mark direction lines with a water-erasable pen. Beware of having stitches at right angles to the design line.

You may find it easiest to start this stitch at the top of a curve or at a point, then to work either side of this.

1. Outline in split stitch (see opposite). Work a straight stitch.

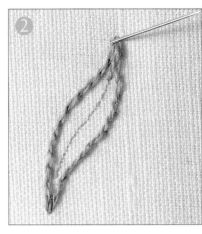

2. Bring the needle up as close as possible to the beginning of the first stitch.

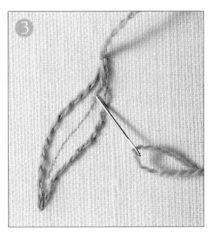

3. Take the needle down near the end of the first stitch.

4. Repeat, angling the stitches to reflect the contour of the design.

The petals on this flower are worked in a split stitch outline, covered with satin stitch.

Coppelia

This section introduces you to five new stitches – fly stitch, buttonhole stitch, detached buttonhole stitch, spider's web stitch and French knots. Using these stitches together brings more texture to this flowing design.

Coppelia

Design size
12 x 21cm (5 x 8½in)

Colours
1 skein each of three shades of blue
1 skein each of three shades of green
1 strand of wool was used throughout

Stitches
The stems are worked in rows of dark green stem stitch and the leaves are worked in fly stitch using all shades of green. The calyxes are worked in dark green spider's web stitch.

The larger flowers use mid-blue buttonhole stitch on the outer edges of the petals, with dark blue detached buttonhole stitch edging. The long edges of the petals are in mid-blue stem stitch and the veins are made up of mid-blue French knots.

The smaller flowers are worked in pale blue buttonhole stitch, stem stitch and French knots. The detached buttonhole edging is in mid-blue.

Fly stitch

Fly stitch is a 'V' stitch. Worked as a solid stitch, it is a very effective way of working leaves, as the centre vein appears as you stitch.

Work this stitch as densely as you would satin stitch. Take care not to make too big a step on the edge or in the centre. In fact, these steps should all be the same size.

If a curved leaf is being worked, it may be necessary to add the odd straight stitch to bring the stitches round on the outside of the curve. It may also be necessary to complete with a little satin stitch.

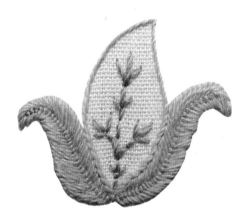

Fly stitch is used to create the veined effect on these leaves.

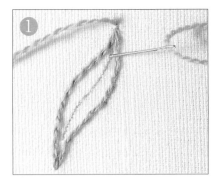

1. Outline the leaf with split stitch. Come up at the point of the leaf, outside the split stitch outline. Make a small straight stitch down the centre line, about 1cm (³⁄₈in) long.

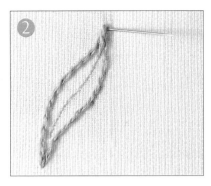

2. Bring the needle up almost beside the beginning of the first stitch, but slightly lower.

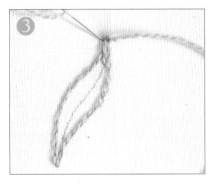

3. Take the needle down on the opposite side of the straight stitch.

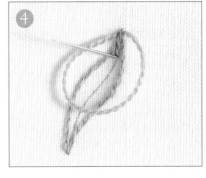

4. Come up at the bottom of the stitch, in the same hole, through the loop.

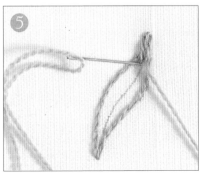

5. Pull the thread taut. Place the needle down at the end of the stitch, stepping below the loop, to make a very small stitch (as if you were finishing a chain stitch).

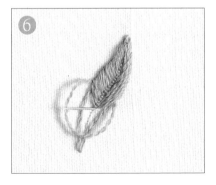

6. Repeat steps 2–5 to build up the stitches and fill in the motif.

Buttonhole stitch

Embroiderers never work blanket stitch . . . or rather they do, but they always call it buttonhole stitch!

If you are right-handed, stitch from left to right, and if left-handed, work from right to left. Keep good tension on the thread at all times and try to work the stitches close together so that no fabric shows between the stitches. When a point or end of a section is reached, finish off with a small stitch outside the loop. Then come back up inside the loop and continue as before.

If you are using buttonhole stitch to add an edge to soft shading, alternate long and short stitches.

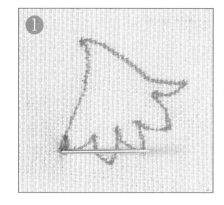

1. Work a straight stitch from the outside in, and bring the needle back up at the first hole.

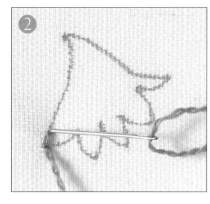

2. Take the needle down beside the end of the first stitch.

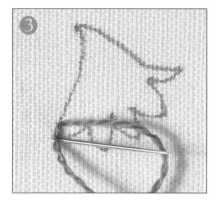

3. Bring the needle up inside the loop, in the design line, beside the first stitch.

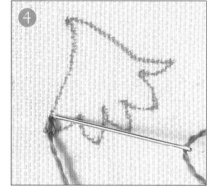

4. Pull the thread taut, keeping the thread level with the fabric. Place the needle down at the side of the beginning of the last stitch.

Buttonhole stitch can be combined with soft shading (see pages 42–43). To do this, work the outer edge of the soft shading in long and short buttonhole stitch then continue in soft shading. This has been used on these pink and blue petals

5. Repeat to outline the motif. To finish, take the needle outside the loop (see page 29, step 5).

Detached buttonhole stitch

This stitch puts a frill on to buttonhole stitch and adds a very effective texture. It is called 'detached' because you do not go through the fabric (except at the beginning or end of a row). When working more than one row, always work in the same direction.

1. Bring the needle up at the beginning of the buttonhole stitch. Pick up the loop at the edge of the buttonhole stitch.

Note Use a tapestry needle to work this stitch.

2. Bring the needle up inside the loop. Pull the thread taut, keeping it level with the fabric.

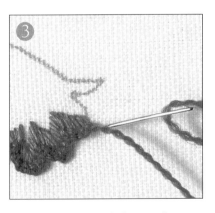

3. Repeat the stitch by stitching into every loop of the buttonhole stitch – this will build up a 'frill'. To finish off, place the needle on the outside of the stitching (see page 29, step 5).

Both these flowers use detached buttonhole stitch. The flower above uses detached buttonhole to add a frill to the centre, and the flower on the right uses detached button hole stitch to add an edge to each set of petals.

Spider's web stitch

This stitch looks like rows of neat bullion knots (see page 44), but it is much more fun to work. I have always thought it should be called Barrister's Wig stitch!

Some rows will be shorter than others, depending on the design shape. The most common problem with this stitch is that not enough rows are worked. Try to ensure that the stitches are packed tightly into an area.

Tension can also cause difficulties – it is best to work slightly looser than usual.

1. Work a central straight stitch in whatever direction required by the design.

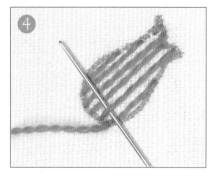

2. Work parallel straight stitches approximately 2.5mm (⅒in) apart, or less, to fill in one side of the motif.

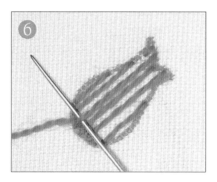

3. Work the other half of the motif. Bring the needle up on one side at the bottom of the motif.

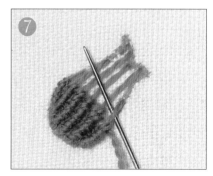

4. Rethread with a tapestry needle. Take the needle under the first straight stitch.

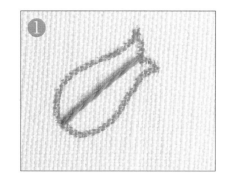

5. Take the needle back over the same straight stitch and under it and the next one.

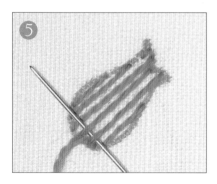

6. Repeat, to fill in a row. Remember that the rule is 'back over one and forward under two'. When you get to the end of the row, only wrap over and under one thread.

7. Take the needle back to the beginning of the row and repeat to fill in the motif. Always work in the same direction.

Circular spider's web stitch

Occasionally, you may want to work a circular area in spider's web stitch (see *Cover Story*, pages 58–63). To do this, you simply lay the straight stitches from the centre of the circle like the spokes of a wheel and then weave as you would normally, spiralling from the centre.

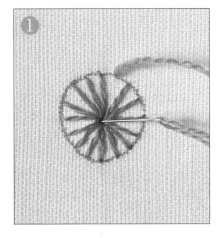

1. Work a circle of straight stitches.

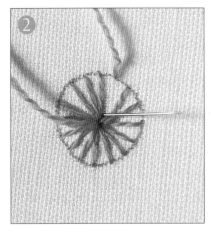

2. Bring your needle up as close to the centre as possible.

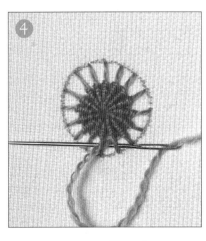

3. Take the needle back over the first stitch, then under it and the next two stitches.

4. Continue, spiralling the stitches round from the centre to complete the circle.

Berries look effective worked in circular spider's web stitch.

37

French knots

This is not a difficult stitch, but I wish I had been taught this method as a small child – it would have saved so many hours of frustration!

If you want a bigger knot, thicken your thread but only wrap it once around the needle. When filling an area solidly with French knots, work around the edge first, then fill in.

French knots are versatile. For example, they can be used for small petals, flower centres, acorns or even grapes (see page 25). French knots are worked with two threads for the flowers above. You could also use two different shades in the needle as in the large coral and gold flowers in the design on the left.

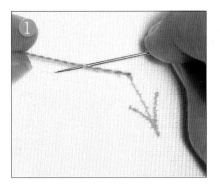

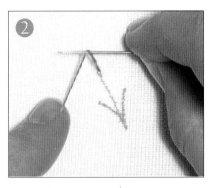

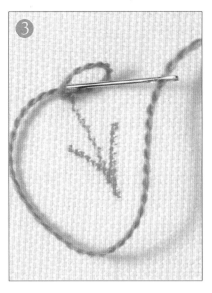

1. Bring the thread to the surface. Pull the thread to the side and take the needle under the thread.

2. Wrap the thread once around the needle, with the needle pointing down.

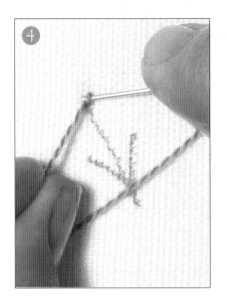

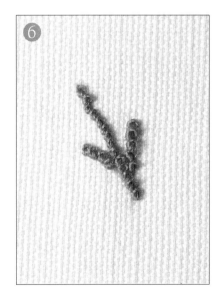

3. Place the needle back down, very close to, but not in, the same hole.

4. Pull the thread taut, taking the knot down on to the fabric.

5. Pull the needle down through the fabric to complete the knot.

6. Repeat to build up a series of French knots.

Sylvia

This section introduces you to
three more stitches – laid
filling, soft shading and
bullion knots. When
combined, they will produce
a completely different effect to
the basic design featured on
page 27.

Sylvia

Design size
12.5 x 21cm (5 x 8½in)

Fabric size
Minimum 25 x 34cm (10 x 13½in)

Colours
*1 skein each of three shades of
cream/yellow*
1 skein each of three shades of green
*1 strand of wool was used
throughout*

Stitches
*The stems, leaves and calyxes are
outlined in green stem stitch.*

*The calyxes are worked in very close
laid filling. The grid is mid-green,
the tying stitch is dark green and the
French knots are pale green.*

*The flowers are worked in soft
shading using pale and mid-cream/
yellow. The bullion knots that form
the veins on the petals are in dark
cream/yellow.*

Laid filling

This very traditional crewel stitch is often referred to in my classes as 'noughts and crosses'. A grid of straight stitches is worked first. These should be very even, but the density of them will depend on the final effect required. Having worked in both directions and achieved beautiful even squares, a small straight stitch or cross stitch is worked across the junction of threads to hold these in place, then a French knot is worked in each square. Generally, the area is then outlined in stem stitch.

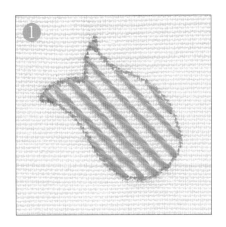

1. Work vertical rows of straight stitch.

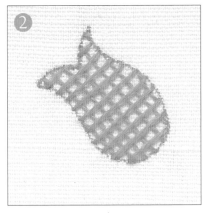

2. Create a grid by working horizontal rows of straight stitch.

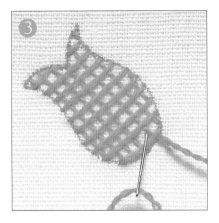

3. Bring the needle up in one of the corners of the grid and work a straight stitch over the junction of threads.

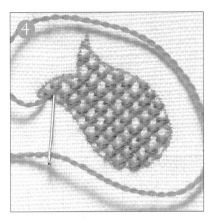

4. Repeat, to secure each junction.

Laid filling works well on leaves. This leaf was first covered with mid-green satin stitch, then the laid filling was worked in light green on top, with dark green tying cross stitches.

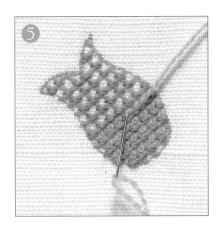

5. Work a French knot in each square (see page 38) to fill in the motif.

Soft shading

Soft shading is traditionally called long and short stitch, but I have adopted Audrey Francini's name for it (*Crewel Embroidery*, published by Van Nostrand Rheinhold in 1979). Long and short sounds regimented, and this stitch should certainly not be that! The method that I show is the traditional method used by the exquisite Chinese embroiderers and The Royal School of Needlework, and it produces a truly blended effect.

Full and part stitches are worked to achieve soft shading. A part stitch is perhaps two thirds of the length of a long stitch. If the first row is worked thickly enough, it is possible to work the following rows openly so the colours bleed through each other.

Do not search for the ends of the shorter stitches, but come up where you would like to see a stitch. Remember that stitches can be overlapped to achieve curves.

It is perfectly acceptable to encroach into a previous colour or row, but you should not work these following rows densely.

There is plenty of opportunity to cheat with this stitch – like jumping back to a worked area and adding the odd stitch to achieve a better effect!

This colourful bird and flower are worked in soft shading to add realism.

1. Outline the area in split stitch. Bring the needle up at the outside of the motif, at a point or top of a curve. Work a straight stitch, 1.25–2cm (½–¾in) in the direction required.

Note If you are working a flower, angle the stitches so they go to the heart of the flower and down the stem.

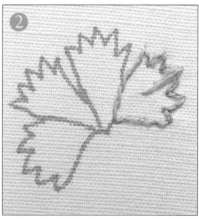

2. Work a part stitch (two thirds the length of the straight stitch).

3. Continue, alternating full and part stitches. Work them extremely close together even overlapping, to make a solid edge.

4. When you have naturally completed an area, bring the needle back to an outside point, and continue working the stitch to fill in the rest of the motif.

5. Take a second colour, close in shade to the first. Take the needle up to split a stitch worked in the first colour, then down past the first colour embroidery to extend the motif.

Note Full and part stitches do not have to be neat and even. Remember that long stitches make smooth work.

Note You can begin the shading anywhere on the first set of stitches.

Note The second and third colours should always be worked up through the embroidery already completed, not down through it.

6. Work straight stitches in the same direction as the first set to create subtle shading. These should not be as close together as the first set.

7. Take a third colour, close in shade to the second. Repeat stages 5 and 6 to fill in the motif.

This bird is worked in a similar way to the one opposite.

Bullion knots

Embroidery is often considered one of the best therapies. However, I am not sure that is true when working this stitch . . .

Note If too many coils are made, this stitch may curve. Sometimes, this might be the effect required.

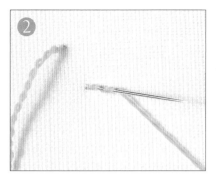

1. Work the needle up through the fabric, then down, leaving a large loop on the surface. The gap between the thread and the needle will determine the length of each stitch.

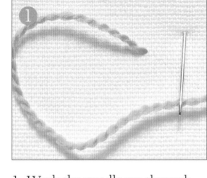

2. Bring the point of the needle back up at the start point. Wrap the wool several times clockwise around the needle.

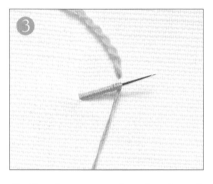

3. Continue wrapping the thread around the needle, until you have a close set of coils the same length as the gap between the two stitch points.

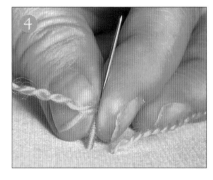

4. Hold the coils with one hand, between thumb and forefinger.

5. With the other hand, gently ease the needle through the coils. Keep calm!

Note If the thread does not move freely, check that there is not a knot on the back.

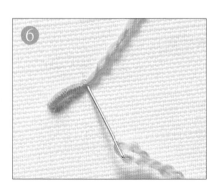

6. Lay the coils down on the fabric and stroke the stitch into place. Secure by taking the thread to the back.

The heart of this flower is worked in a cluster of mid-gold and dark gold bullion knots.

Allium

This panel uses a variety of stitches, including those featured in the book, with the exception of detached buttonhole and spider's web. It is suitable for a picture, cushion, seat or stool top. It could also be used as a pole screen.

Les Sylphides

Design size
37 x 21cm (15 x 8½in)

Colours
1 skein of pale pink

2 skeins each of mid- and dark pink, pale and dark green

3 skeins of mid-green

1 strand of wool was used throughout

Stitches
Follow the instructions for the individual carnation projects. Working from left to right, embroider Giselle, then Sylvia in the centre and Coppelia on the right. The arrangement of the shades of thread is as in the original three panels, but where yellow and blue are used, substitute pink.

An alternative suggestion
You could work a bell-pull using five repeats of the design stacked on top of each other and touching. From top to bottom use the designs in this order: Giselle, Sylvia, Coppelia, Sylvia, Giselle. The finished design size would be 12.5 x 105cm (5 x 42½in).

Finale

Throughout this book I have not discussed uses for the projects. This has been deliberate. People so often look at a design and may discard it because, for instance, they do not like cushions! Hopefully, by showing only the design, you can apply your own imagination when deciding how to use the finished pieces. Crewel embroidery is great for stools, chair seats, cushions, curtains, curtain borders or pelmets, bedspreads, waistcoats, boxes, bell pulls, panels, bags and even pictures. However, there is one very important process to work through before making up: the stretching or blocking process (both terms are used widely to describe the same thing).

Tanglewood bell pull

Woodland creatures and birds look very effective when worked in crewel embroidery.

Stretching

Before stretching your finished piece, you need to decide whether to wash it first. I happily wash all my needlework, my husband's suits and our winter coats! I have even washed a canvas embroidered cushion, still with its feather pad inside! As my embroidery is made up of linen, cotton and wool, I use the wool cycle on my automatic washing machine with my normal washing powder. I give it a good spin and then leave it to dry by a radiator. Then it is ready for stretching.

Stretching is one of the great exciting moments of crewel embroidery, as the starches from the linen bring sparkle back to the fabric. I sometimes also find this a sad moment as I often regret finishing something I have so enjoyed stitching!

1. Cover the board with dressmaker's graph paper. Secure in place with masking tape.

2. Remove any edge binding from the finished embroidery. Make sure the fabric is straight in line with a thread of the fabric. Place the embroidery right side up on top of the board. Line up one of the edges with a line on the graph paper.

3. Hammer in a nail every 2cm (¾in) along one of the sides. Repeat along an adjacent side. Try to work about 1.25cm (½in) from the raw edge of the fabric, keeping the edge of the fabric in line with a line on the graph paper.

Note Pull firmly as you nail, so that the material is taut but not over-stretched.

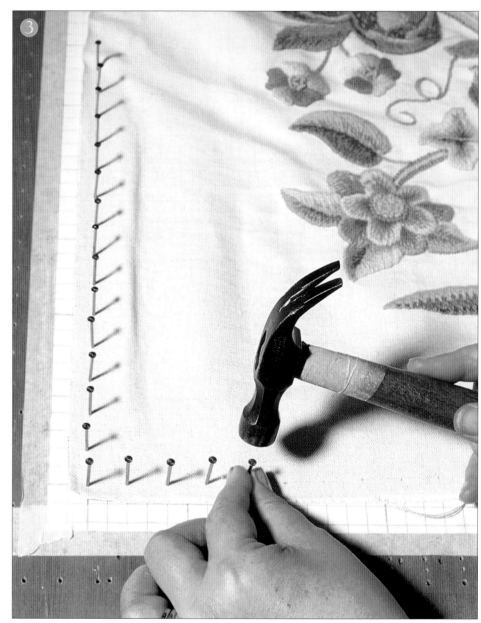

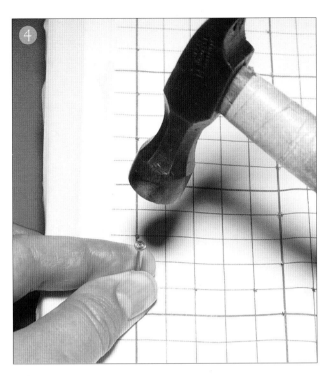

4. Turn the board around. Use the graph paper and the two completed sides as a guide to place holes along the other two sides, where you will eventually put the nails.

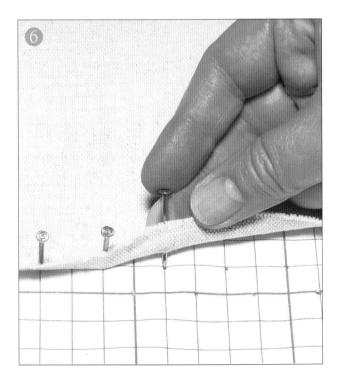

5. Pull out the fourth corner, diagonally opposite the first, so that it is square. Hammer in the corner nail, then two further nails to support the corner.

Note If you cannot get the fourth corner square, remove the nails down the side, leaving the nails in the three corners. Now have another go!

6. Gently push a nail through the fabric, then ease it into one of the holes made in step 4. Tap with a hammer to secure the nail. Repeat, to stretch the remaining two sides. The work should now be very square and firmly stretched.

7. Dampen the embroidery and fabric using a mist sprayer filled with water. Alternatively, use a wet sponge.

> *Note* Once you have stretched your piece, you can leave your graph paper in place, ready to stretch your next piece of embroidery. The graph paper in this demonstration has been used several times!

8. Stand the board somewhere warm to dry. When dry, remove all nails.

> *Note* You can stand the board up against a radiator to dry, place it in the airing cupboard or, if you are in a desperate hurry, a hair dryer is very useful. Do not leave the work wet and nailed out for too long as rust from the nails could damage the fabric. I have also known of mould growing on a finished piece. To avoid disappointment, as soon as the work is thoroughly dry, remove all the nails.

Arcadia

This is a traditional tree of life design, found worked in many different styles over the centuries. This panel would be perfect as a picture or firescreen.

Gallery

The two designs in this section combine all the stitches you have learnt. The first, Flutterby, was inspired by typical Elizabethan scrolling designs. The second, Cover Story, by a Georgian stool covered with canvas embroidery. I hope that now you have learnt the basic stitches, you will have the confidence to go on and develop your skills and experiment with different designs.

Flutterby

Design size

20 x 20cm (8 x 8in)

Colours

1 skein each of: three shades of pink; three shades of blue; three shades of mauve; three shades of gold; three shades of mid-green; three shades of pale green

1 strand of wool was used throughout

Stitches

The stem is worked in one line of dark green chain stitch. This is outlined on one side only with mid-green stem stitch. The tendrils are also worked in mid-green stem stitch.

The butterfly's head and body are in dark gold satin stitch. Its legs and antennae are in dark gold stem stitch. The upper wing and outer bands are in dark and pale pink satin stitch. The inner area is worked in soft shading, using all three shades of mauve. The outer band of the lower wing is dark pink buttonhole stitch and the spots are dark pink satin stitch surrounded by rows of pale pink stem stitch. The inner section is worked in soft shading, using all three shades of blue.

The upper petals on the bottom left flower are worked in mid-pink and pale pink fly stitch. The flower centre is worked in shaded spider's web using all three golds. The mauve section is worked in rows of French knots using all three shades of mauve. The lower petals are worked in soft shading and all three shades of pink. The bottom pair of leaves are worked in mid-green and dark green fly stitch.

The centre of the flower in the top left is worked in dark gold French knots. The inner petals are worked in soft shading, using pale and mid-gold. The outer petals are outlined in mid-blue buttonhole stitch and have a frill of dark blue detached buttonhole stitch. They are filled with French knots, with rows worked from outside in pale blue, pale and mid-mauve filled with dark mauve. The leaflets are in dark green bullion knots.

The petals on the bottom right hand flower are worked in satin stitch in all three shades of blue. The calyx is in laid filling using all three shades of green – the grid is in dark green, the tying stitch is in mid-green and the French knots are in pale green. Pale gold French knots are used to form the stamens, with fine stems in mid-gold stem stitch, and the heavier stem in dark gold chain stitch. The leaf above this flower is worked using soft shading and all three shades of green. The inner dark shade has been worked as fly stitch.

The centre of the flower in the top right is worked in soft shading, using all three shades of mauve, with top stitching in dark gold. The petals either side of this are in pale and mid-pink soft shading. The lower petals are in rows of stem stitch which use all three shades of pink. The leaves are in dark green fly stitch and the calyx is in dark green spider's web stitch.

Details taken from Flutterby, featured on page 54

Pattern for Flutterby

Cover story

Design size
25 x 39cm (10 x 15½in)

Colours
1 skein each of three shades of pink; three shades of coral; three shades of blue; three shades of gold; three shades of yellow; three shades of fawn; three shades of turquoise; pale green; dark olive green

2 skeins each of mid-green; dark green; pale olive green; mid-olive green

One strand of wool was used throughout, except for eight areas of French knots where two strands of wool were used.

Stitches
See page 60.

Stitches

All stems are worked in rows of fawn stem stitch, and all leaves are worked in fly stitch using all three shades of green, turquoise and olive. The small yellow flower on the bottom left, and similar ones in the top centre and far right, are worked in mid-yellow and dark yellow satin stitch.

Their centres are made up of French knots, with straight stitches to the edge, in two steps in dark gold.

The larger flower in the bottom left hand corner has outer petals in soft shading using all three shades of blue. The middle area is worked in shaded spider's web stitch using all three shades of pink. Mid-pink is used for the spokes. The heart of the flower is in mid-gold and dark gold bullion knots.

The small flowers to the right of this are worked in pale yellow, mid-gold and dark gold satin stitch. The calyxes are in dark turquoise satin stitch.

The terracotta flower to the right of this has petals worked in soft shading, using all three shades of coral soft shading. The inner area is filled with French knots using pale yellow and all three shades of gold; two strands of wool were used for these. The calyxes are in dark olive chain stitch.

Further to the right is a group of blue flowers whose petals are worked in satin stitch using all three shades of blue. Their centres are filled with mid-gold French knots using two strands of wool. Their leaflets are worked in pale and mid-olive fly stitch.

The flower on the far bottom right has its centre worked in dark yellow circular spider's web stitch. The petals are worked in soft shading, using all three shades of pink.

The small flowers above this are in all three shades of gold and satin stitch, with calyxes in dark turquoise satin stitch.

The star flower to the left of these has a centre of dark gold French knots (one strand) surrounded by mid-yellow satin stitch. The outer petals are worked in mid-coral buttonhole soft shading (see page 34), with a pale coral detached buttonhole frill. They are filled with dark coral soft shading.

The central flower has petals worked in laid filling using all three shades of blue – mid for the grid, dark for the tying stitch and pale for the French knots. These petals are outlined in dark pink chain stitch. The inner petals are worked in mid-pink buttonhole stitch, with a pale pink detached buttonhole frill. The centre is worked in mid-pink and dark pink bullion knots and pale and dark pink French knots.

The flower on the far left has leaflets in mid-olive satin stitch. The petals are in mid-coral buttonhole stitch, with pale coral detached buttonhole frills. They are filled with dark coral French knots (one strand).

The small flowers at the top are similar to their counterparts below. The pink flowers are all worked in French Knots (one strand) using pale coral and all three shades of pink.

The flower at the top right has a circular spider's web in the centre worked in mid-yellow, with a little dark yellow shading on the upper side. The petals are worked in all three shades of blue satin stitch.

Pattern for Cover story

For ease of photocopying, this pattern has been split into two. Photocopy each piece separately, then match up the central flower and join the two pieces with invisible tape. Remember that you can enlarge the design when you photocopy it, to make it whatever size you require.

Index